WHAT DO YOU KNOW ABOUT

Drugs

PETE SANDERS and STEVE MYERS

Gloucester Press
LONDON • SYDNEY

© Aladdin Books Ltd 1995

All rights reserved

Designed and produced by
Aladdin Books Ltd
28 Percy Street
London W1P 0LD

First published in Great Britain in 1995 by Watts Books
96 Leonard Street
London EC2A 4RH

ISBN: 0 7496 2097 8

A catalogue record for this book is available from the British Library.

Printed in Belgium

Design	David West Children's Book Design
Editor	Sarah Levete
Picture research	Brooks Krikler Research
Illustrator	Mike Lacy

Pete Sanders is Senior Lecturer in health education at the University of North London. He was a head teacher for ten years and has written many books on social issues for children.

Steve Myers is a freelance writer. He has co-written other titles in this series and has worked on several educational projects for children.

The consultant, Adrian King, is a health education co-ordinator for a local education authority. He has worked as a teacher and youth and community worker.

CONTENTS

HOW TO USE THIS BOOK..................2
INTRODUCTION.................3
WHAT ARE DRUGS?..................4
DIFFERENT KINDS OF DRUGS..................7
WHY DO PEOPLE MISUSE DRUGS?..................12
DRUGS AND SOCIETY..................15
ADDICTION AND DEPENDENCY..................18
WHAT DRUG-TAKING CAN LEAD TO..................21
KICKING THE HABIT..................24
WHAT CAN BE DONE ABOUT DRUG ABUSE?..................27
WHAT CAN WE DO?..................30
INDEX..................32

HOW TO USE THIS BOOK
The books in this series are intended to help young people to understand more about issues that may affect their lives.

Each book can be read by a child alone, or together with a parent, teacher or helper. Issues raised in the storyline are further discussed in the accompanying text, so that there is an opportunity to talk through ideas as they come up.

At the end of the book there is a section called "What Can We Do?". This gives practical ideas which will be useful for both young people and adults. Organisations and helplines are also listed, to provide the reader with additional sources of information and support.

INTRODUCTION

AT SOME TIME IN OUR LIVES, ALL OF US WILL COME INTO CONTACT WITH SOME FORM OF DRUG.

Drugs can be extremely useful. Some are vital in helping people who are ill. However, abuse of certain drugs has become a major problem for both individuals and society.

This book will help you to understand more about drugs and the dangers of drug abuse. Each chapter introduces a different aspect of the subject, illustrated by a continuing storyline. The characters in the story have to deal with situations which you might have to face yourself at some point in your life. After each episode, we stop and look at the issues raised, and widen out the discussion.

By the end, you will know more about the different kinds of drugs and why some people misuse drugs. You will also understand the effects that drugs can have on a person's life, what can be done to help drug users and to stop the illegal use of drugs.

WHAT ARE DRUGS?

A DRUG IS A SUBSTANCE WHICH, WHEN TAKEN INTO A PERSON'S BODY, ALTERS OR INTERFERES WITH THE WAY IN WHICH THE BODY FUNCTIONS.

This effect may be helpful. Doctors prescribe all kinds of drugs to treat different illnesses. If used incorrectly, however, drugs can be dangerous.

Drugs have been around in different forms for hundreds of years. Some are natural remedies. Others are produced from plants or are manufactured in laboratories. You are probably aware of many of them – perhaps you have drunk coffee, or taken a tablet for a headache. The most widely used drugs today are tobacco and alcohol.

Not all drugs have the same use or effect. Some are used to treat illnesses, helping the body to repair itself or helping to prevent disease. Others may be taken because people believe that they will have a pleasurable effect. Some drugs are much more powerful than others. One drug may come in different forms and strengths. The effect of a particular drug may also differ from person to person. It can depend upon factors such as a person's size, age and general state of health. If someone is not used to a particular drug, the effect may be stronger than on someone whose body has become used to the drug. One person may be able to drink a lot of alcohol without appearing drunk. Another may drink a small amount and still become very drunk.

Many people enjoy an alcoholic drink, a cigarette or a cup of coffee. These are all forms of drugs.

What Are Drugs?

The doctors are giving Mrs Young pills to help make her well.
A medicine is a drug or combination of drugs which has been designed to treat a particular illness. Some can be bought from chemists and other shops. Others are prescribed by doctors, and may contain very powerful drugs.

When a doctor prescribes a medicine for a patient, he or she is taking into account several factors, including any possible side effects that a medicine may have on the patient. It is important that you never take a medicine which has been prescribed for somebody else, even if you think you have the same symptoms. Doing so can be very dangerous. If you do feel unwell, tell your parent or carer.

Taking more than the recommended dosage of medicine can be harmful.
Unlike most medicines, some drugs such as cigarettes, coffee and alcohol do not give a dosage on the packet or bottle. But this does not mean that you can have as much of them as you want without any negative effect.

Lisa is worried that her mum may have to take the pills for a long time.
Some people need to take a particular medicine for the rest of their lives. Some doctors have been criticised for prescribing too many drugs unnecessarily. Or they have been accused of repeating a prescription for a patient, without checking to make sure the person still needs the drug.

Different Kinds of Drugs

THERE ARE HUNDREDS OF DIFFERENT DRUGS. THEY COME IN VARIOUS FORMS. SOMETIMES THEY ARE POWDERS OR TABLETS. THEY MIGHT BE LIQUIDS OR EVEN DRIED PLANTS.

Prescribed or legally obtainable drugs are produced to carefully controlled standards of quality. There are no such safeguards with drugs which are produced, bought or used illegally.

The effect that a drug has on a person depends on the type of drug, its strength and how much is taken. It can also be influenced by the method of taking the drug, the situation in which it is taken, the health of the person and his or her motive for taking it. Sometimes, people take more than one drug to achieve a particular effect. These drug 'cocktails' can be very dangerous. Different combinations will affect people in different ways. At the end of this chapter is information about the most commonly used and abused drugs. It shows some of their possible effects, though these will not always be the same for everyone. It also gives details of some of the possible problems associated with each drug.

Drugs which are prescribed by doctors for medicinal purposes are produced and tested under strictly controlled conditions.

Different Kinds Of Drugs

ALCOHOL • Often drunk as beer, wine or spirits • Relaxing effect • Too much will make people 'drunk' • Side-effects: 'hangover' – nausea, headaches, trembling • Acts as a depressant – slowing down the body's reactions • Lessens user's control over emotions & behaviour • Can cause damage to the nervous system & liver • Can be addictive • Many deaths each year from alcohol abuse • Legal in many countries but laws control the age at which it can be bought

AMPHETAMINES • Stimulate the body's nervous system and increase blood pressure • Usually taken by mouth – sometimes injected or sniffed • User may feel alert, confident • Can reduce the desire for sleep • Continued usage can lead to irritability; inability to sleep; anxiety; a fear of others • Also known as whizz, speed, uppers, sulphate • Illegal to sell or possess • Can be prescribed by doctors

AMYL NITRITE • Clear liquid, used medically to treat heart conditions • Usually supplied in a small bottle • Vapour is sniffed through the nose • Also known as poppers • Causes increase in temperature & heartbeat, giving a short-lived feeling of well-being • Continued use can cause dizziness & headaches • Excessive use may lead to blackouts and vomiting • Currently legal

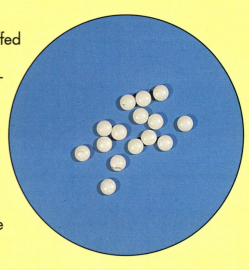

ANABOLIC STEROIDS • Powerful hormones • May be prescribed by doctors for medical conditions • Used by some sportspeople who believe they improve performance • Can have serious and irreversible side-effects on user's reproductive system if not taken under medical supervision • Not illegal to possess, but are a 'prescription only' drug

BARBITURATES & OTHER DEPRESSANTS • Slow down certain body functions • Can have relaxing effect & may appear to reduce stress • Long-term use can lead to depression; forgetfulness; increased aggression; an inability to sleep without them; breathing difficulties • Examples of barbiturates include Seconal and Tuinol • Overdose can kill, particularly if taken after alcohol • Tranquillisers are milder depressants – also called tranx – examples include Librium and Valium • All depressants can be very addictive • Most can be possessed legally, if prescribed

CAFFEINE • Drug contained in coffee & other drinks, including tea & some soft drinks such as cola • Mild addictive stimulant • Can cause increased heartbeat; heartburn; sleeplessness; stomach upsets

Different Kinds Of Drugs

CANNABIS • Usually smoked or may be eaten • Comes in solid or leaf form • Also known as marijuana, pot, hash, grass, dope, joint, spliff & reefer • Can cause feeling of well-being & relaxation • High dosages can cause vomiting & diarrhoea • Continued use can affect people's memory & concentration • Can cause lung damage when smoked • Illegal in most countries to possess or sell

COCAINE • Fine, white powder • Sniffed or injected • Also known as coke or snow • May create a feeling of well-being & increased energy • Effect wears off quickly – users may take another dose to try to maintain the 'high' • If sniffed over a long period, can damage the inside of the nose • Large doses can lead to breathing difficulties and occasionally death • Crack cocaine comes in solid pea-sized lumps which are heated & the smoke inhaled • Known as freebase cocaine, rock or wash • Frequent use of cocaine or crack cocaine can cause exhaustion, nervousness & hallucinations • Illegal to possess or sell

ECSTASY • Tablet or capsule form • Known as E or disco biscuits • Effects include: brief feeling of sickness; increased heart rate; a feeling of calm; greater awareness of surroundings • Has been popular on dance & rave scene • Causes body to sweat more – loss of fluid, together with the heat of dancing, can cause heatstroke – this can be fatal • Side-effects include: diarrhoea; tiredness; depression • Illegal to possess or sell

HEROIN • Usually a brownish powder • Either smoked or dissolved & injected • Known as smack, skag or H • First effects include feeling of warmth & pleasure • Addictive if used over a period of time • Withdrawal causes vomiting, aches, sweating & tiredness • Dangers from overdose & injecting the impurities which are almost always mixed with street-bought drugs • Possession or sale of heroin is illegal • May be prescribed by doctors medically

LSD • Pill form or as a small piece of blotting paper or sugar cube containing the LSD • Causes hallucinations & altered sense of reality • Effects can be very unpredictable – some 'trips' may be unpleasant • Can cause depression; anxiety; panic attacks; dizziness • Also known as acid, trips, tabs • Illegal to sell or possess

NICOTINE • The drug in tobacco • Can be very addictive • Tobacco comes in leaf form – made into cigarettes or cigars, used in pipes or sniffed as 'snuff' • Smoking can cause many illnesses, including cancer & heart disease • Legal to possess tobacco • Illegal for shopkeepers to sell cigarettes to people below a certain age

SOLVENTS, GAS & GLUE • Effects of inhaling vapours of glue, varnishes & lighter fuel can include: dizziness; hallucinations; short-lived feeling of well-being • Can cause nausea; tiredness; headaches • Can cause death from lack of oxygen; inhaling vomit • Legal to possess these products • Illegal for shops to sell them, if they suspect they will be sniffed

WHY DO PEOPLE MISUSE DRUGS?

THERE IS NO ONE SIMPLE EXPLANATION WHY PEOPLE TAKE DRUGS WHEN THEY DO NOT MEDICALLY NEED TO DO SO.

For many people, the reason is the promise of the 'high'. The high is brought about by the drug and changes the way a person feels or views the world.

This can be an intense feeling of well-being, and may be pleasurable. Because drugs alter the way people feel, they can become a way of escaping temporarily from emotions or situations which are difficult to cope with. Other people may decide to take a drug because they are curious about the drug's effect and want to experience it for themselves. Or it may just be that drugs are easily available.

Wanting to fit in as part of a group can be a strong influence. If others are putting pressure on you to do something, it can be difficult to refuse, even if you want to. Sometimes people have used drugs as the result of a dare. Or they may do it as a form of rebellion, or simply because they believe drug-taking will be fun.

Whatever people's reasons for starting to take drugs, they may not always be aware of what their decision could lead to. Abuse of drugs has the potential to affect your life and health seriously.

Some people take drugs because their 'friends' do. They may be worried about what the 'friends' will think if they refuse. It takes courage to say no.

The others are putting pressure on Chrissie to smoke the 'joint'.
Everyone forms their own opinions of what is right and wrong. If you are part of a larger group, it can be hard to say what you think. If everyone is doing the opposite of what you want or believe is right, it can be tempting to go along with them. It is not always easy to stand up for yourself. It helps to think things through before making a decision. How would you deal with a situation where drugs are on offer and you felt under pressure to do the same as other people?

Like Josh, many people who take drugs think that they will be able to control their behaviour.
But this is rarely the case. People who have tried drugs may think there are no long-term physical or emotional effects. Or they may believe that somehow they are different – that nothing can harm them. But the reality is that drugs can harm anyone who takes them.

New experiences are part of life.
Trying out different things can be great fun. Some drugs can make you feel good or different for a short while, but there are other long-term and more serious effects which need to be considered. Putting yourself at risk by experimenting, as Chrissie and Josh are doing, is not sensible. It is important to understand the possible consequences of your decisions and actions.

DRUGS AND SOCIETY

THE WAY PEOPLE THINK AND FEEL ABOUT DRUG-TAKING VARIES A GREAT DEAL.

Some believe that the laws about taking certain drugs should be less severe. Others think that legislation is not strict enough.

Sometimes illegal drug-taking is viewed as a problem that happens only in big cities or only to certain groups of people. This is not so. People from all walks of life, of all ages, and from a range of backgrounds can become drug users. Drug abuse is a world-wide problem which affects many areas of society.

Supplying drugs has become very big business. The movement of drugs between countries – 'trafficking' – is very risky. Drug traffickers set up very complicated systems, using sophisticated equipment, in order to make their enormous profits. This may involve bribery of officials and even the use of violence. Most countries have very strict laws with high penalties for those convicted.

Different types of drugs have different images. In many countries, alcohol is widely used in social situations. The fact that it is a very powerful drug is often overlooked. Nicotine is a very addictive drug but it is also legal and easily available. Ecstasy has become popular with dancers at raves. Cocaine is often thought of as a 'trendy' drug.

Pop and movie stars are sometimes criticised for giving the impression that illegal drugs are acceptable. But nobody is immune to their dangers. River Phoenix died from a drugs overdose.

Some sportsmen and women have taken drugs to help them win.
They believe that certain drugs may make them stronger or enable them to run faster. This gives them an unfair advantage over their rivals. At most large competitions athletes are tested for a wide variety of different drugs. If they are found to have used drugs to try to improve their performance, they may be banned from the sport. The most common drugs used in this way are called 'anabolic steroids'. These can have dangerous side-effects.

People like Frank, who make money from selling drugs illegally, are called 'dealers'.
They are also know as 'pushers' or 'suppliers'. Buying drugs from a dealer is very risky. There is no control over the quality of the drug being bought. Dealers may increase the price they charge as the buyer takes the drug more regularly. People can run up huge debts and may turn to crime to pay for their drugs. Dealers may become violent with people who cannot pay.

Most countries have laws about drugs.
These laws may differ from place to place. In the UK, Australia and the USA, it is a crime to possess any illegal drug, even if you do not intend to sell it. Alcohol is illegal in some Muslim countries. In Holland and some other countries, people are allowed to buy and sell certain drugs such as cannabis.

ADDICTION AND DEPENDENCY

MANY PEOPLE FIND IT DIFFICULT TO STOP TAKING DRUGS, BECAUSE THEY HAVE COME TO DEPEND ON THE EFFECT OF THE DRUGS THEY ARE TAKING.

Some drugs are physically addictive, causing changes in the body which produce a need for the drug. However, dependence on the feelings that some drugs create, or on the lifestyle and sense of freedom that some people believe they offer, can be just as powerful. If the body has come to depend on the drug, it may crave more of it. Unpleasant sensations – withdrawal symptoms – are felt when the drug is not being taken or when its effects are wearing off. These can be very serious. With some drugs the body develops a tolerance, adapting itself so that a higher dose may be needed to produce the same effect. But this does not mean that the user's body becomes immune to the physical dangers of the drug.

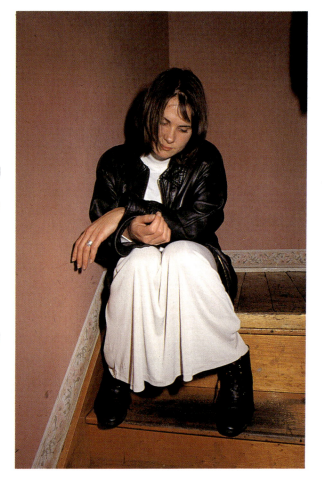

People who use drugs to cope with difficult situations or to relieve unhappiness may become caught up in a pattern. For a short while, the drug will take away the painful emotions but afterwards people may feel even worse. The physical effects of the drug wearing off can make people feel unhappy. There may also be a sense of guilt and shame. If they cannot deal with this they may turn again to drugs to escape from their feelings.

Some drugs are much more addictive than others. It is unlikely that anybody who starts to take drugs expects to become addicted. For smokers, the addiction to the nicotine in the cigarettes may become the only reason that they continue to smoke them. The only way to be sure of avoiding addiction is not to experiment with drugs.

Ethan believes that he is in control.
One of the effects of taking some drugs is to make people unable to think clearly. Their reactions to situations and their ability to reason or to make sensible judgements may be affected. Drugs such as LSD, cannabis and alcohol can alter people's sense of reality. They may feel powerful and no longer appear to sense pain. Under the influence of drugs, some users have attempted very dangerous activities and believe that they can do impossible things like fly.

Some drug users inject the substance into their veins.
Unskilled injecting is dangerous. It can lead to infections or collapsed veins. If drug users inject with needles that are dirty, they may also be injecting germs into their body, along with the drug. Sharing needles can transfer tiny drops of one person's blood to the other person. If the blood is infected, the infection is also transferred. This is one way in which HIV, the virus which can lead to AIDS, is transmitted. In some countries there are needle exchanges where drug users can discard used needles safely and collect clean needles, unlike in the photo (left). This may reduce the risks from using dirty needles, but it does not help to prevent any of the other dangers associated with taking illegal drugs.

Ethan's parents have noticed that his behaviour has changed.
The craving for drugs can take over a person's life, affecting both the drug user and those who are close to him or her. But it can take a long time for others to become aware that a person is dependent on drugs.

WHAT DRUG-TAKING CAN LEAD TO

AS WELL AS THE DEVASTATING EFFECT SOME DRUGS CAN HAVE ON THE BODY, DRUG-TAKING CAN CAUSE OTHER PROBLEMS.

Many drugs alter the way that people behave and can distort their thinking. This can lead to drug users becoming a danger, both to themselves and to other people.

This is one reason why there are strict laws about not driving or operating machinery under the influence of alcohol or other drugs. Depending on the drug taken, the immediate effects might include feelings of power or pleasure. However, there can be serious long-term physical and emotional effects of continued drug abuse. In some cases, drug abuse can lead to death.

Heavy drug users may seem to care more about their drug-taking than about the people who are close to them. This can lead to the break-up of relationships. Friends and relatives may experience a great deal of stress and worry.

If someone is found guilty of possessing even a small amount of illegal drugs by the police, he or she will then have a criminal record for life.

Obtaining drugs illegally can be very expensive. Some drug addicts may turn to stealing, and sometimes prostitution, in order to get the money they need for their supply of drugs.

What Drug-Taking Can Lead To

▽ When Lisa arrived home, she went straight to Josh's room and told him what had happened.

▷ The next day at school, Chrissie went looking for Josh. She was supposed to go with him to a party but had decided not to.

▽ Chrissie had realised how much the drugs had taken over her life. She wanted to stop.

△ Josh said he couldn't. He begged Lisa not to say anything until he'd had a chance to try and sort things out.

▽ There was a shout from behind the two boys. Tanya had collapsed.

▷ At the party, Josh offered to pay off his debt a little at a time. Frank just laughed at him.

What Drug-Taking Can Lead To

Some people think that a person who experiments with a drug such as cannabis will eventually go on to try other, more addictive, drugs. Others believe this is not the case. The truth is that it is likely to be different for different people.

However, if you have taken one drug, it may be tempting to try another.

This is why it is important to think about what the results of taking any drug might be and to know about the risks involved.

Josh is worried about the effect the drug has had on Tanya.
Illegally produced drugs are not screened for safety. There are no guarantees of purity or strength. The drug that you think you are buying may not be what you are actually given. Taking these drugs is extremely risky. The effect you anticipated may be very different from what happens. It is possible to overdose on drugs. This is when a person has taken too much of a particular drug too quickly. The effects of an overdose can be devastating. It can result in death.

Dealers may take advantage of the drug user's craving and their need for the drug.
They know that many users will not only come to depend on the drug itself, but will also rely on their dealer to supply it. Dealers also need customers. They can be ruthless in the way that they tempt people into starting to take drugs, and then encourage them to continue their drug habit. This can involve people in difficult and even dangerous situations.

KICKING THE HABIT

NO ONE STARTS TO TAKE DRUGS INTENDING TO MAKE IT A HABIT. NO ONE EXPECTS TO BECOME DEPENDENT ON DRUGS. COMING OFF DRUGS CAN BE A LONG AND DIFFICULT PROCESS.

Realising that you have a problem, and owning up to it, is not easy. Doing something about it can be even harder. But people can and do stop taking drugs.

People are often frightened of what this might mean. For a long time, they may continue to deny that there is a problem. Most people need a lot of help to be able to do without the drug they have come to depend on. Life may suddenly seem very empty without it. Giving up the drug might involve giving up a lifestyle that the person has become used to.

There are various ways that drug users can get the help they need. Some people spend time in hospital; others may join self-help groups or receive counselling. Sometimes people may not be able to come off the drug completely at once – it may even be dangerous to try. Under medical supervision, drug therapy may be used to substitute a different drug or to give a lower dose of the same one. In this way, the amount of the drug being taken can be reduced gradually and safely, without the drug-taker experiencing severe withdrawal symptoms.

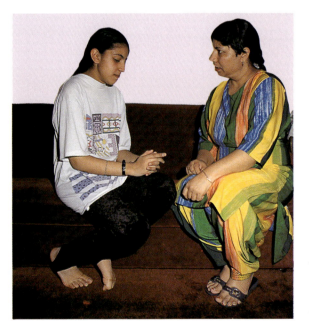

Telling someone that you have a problem with drugs is a difficult but brave step to take. It can mean coming to terms with feelings that the drug-taking has temporarily blotted out.

Ethan is upset by what has happened to Tanya. It has made him aware of the risks and the dangers involved in drug-taking.

A person's decision to seek help with a drug problem may depend on different factors. Sometimes, it can take a shock to make people understand how serious the situation has become.

Ethan has now realised that he is the only person who can change his behaviour. He has refused to go along with Sam. It can take a great deal of courage to stand up and face a problem, especially if you know that it will involve some pain and will not be easy. But it is never too late to decide to give up drugs. Believing in yourself is often the first step. Seeking help when you need it is a wise thing to do.

A person who is taking drugs may already be experiencing feelings of guilt or shame. Blaming someone for taking drugs will not help that person to get better, and will probably make the situation worse.

Sometimes giving support to people who are recovering from drug addiction might mean being tough on them. They may appear to be in great distress. They could even beg to be given the drug or money to buy it. Saying no to them may not be easy – at the time they may become angry or abusive. But later they will be grateful for your support.

WHAT CAN BE DONE ABOUT DRUG ABUSE?

THERE ARE MANY DIFFERENT WAYS IN WHICH PEOPLE ARE TRYING TO STOP DRUGS BEING ABUSED.

It may never be possible to stop the supply of illegal drugs completely. So, as well as trying to make them less available, measures are also being taken to reduce the demand for them.
Education is important in doing this. The more that people – particularly young people – know about the dangers of drugs, the less likely they might be to experiment with them. Education can also help to build self-esteem and enable you to be more assertive if you are faced with a situation in which you are being tempted to use drugs. There are many organisations which exist to help and support people with drug problems to come off the drug. Today, there is also more awareness about the need to stop some forms of drug-taking from appearing glamorous. Some pop and film stars are involved in campaigns which help people to understand more about the dangers involved in drug-taking.

In many countries cigarette and alcohol advertising has been restricted.

Many countries have special police forces whose job it is to catch those who are trafficking in and supplying drugs. But illegal drug-taking continues to be a huge problem throughout the world.

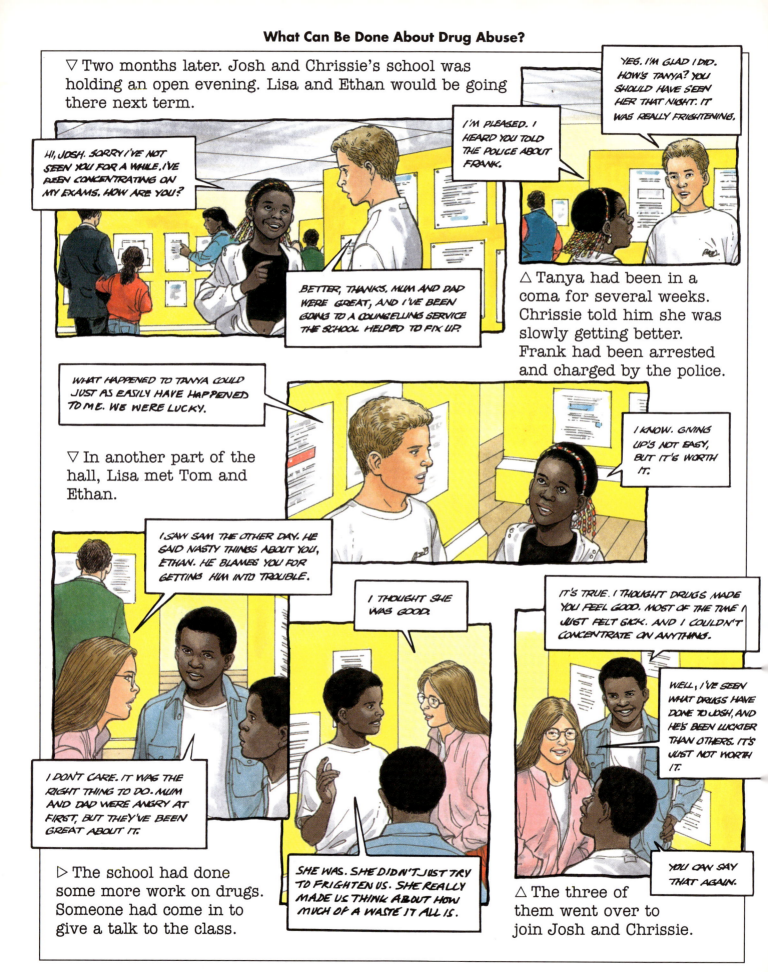

What Can Be Done About Drug Abuse?

Drugs can have a devastating effect on people's lives – and not just the drug taker's.
If you are tempted to take drugs when you do not need to do so for medical reasons, remember that the effect you might get from them will not last and it may not be entirely pleasant. The long-term physical and emotional effects can be extremely serious.

Whatever the problem you are faced with, it helps to talk to somebody about it.
It is important to choose somebody whom you can trust, and to whom you feel comfortable talking. If you think that somebody is dealing in drugs, or has a drug problem, it may be best to tell someone, though this might not be easy, especially if the person is a friend. Speaking out could help to save someone's life.

Learning how to stand up for your rights is a good way of protecting yourself.
Some schools have invited former drug users to talk to pupils about their experiences. Some schools give young people the chance to practise how they will refuse drugs, if they are ever offered them.

You always have the right to say no to drugs.

WHAT CAN WE DO?

HAVING READ THIS BOOK, YOU WILL NOW UNDERSTAND MORE ABOUT THE DIFFERENT KINDS OF DRUGS, AND THE EFFECTS THEY CAN HAVE ON PEOPLE.

All drugs can cause problems. Tobacco smoking has been linked to many major diseases, and alcohol abuse can do serious damage to people's lives.

Growing up is a time of many changes. You may be keen to try new things. People might suggest that taking drugs will make you seem more grown-up. You know that this is not the case. It is important to recognise when situations may arise in which drugs could be around. You might want to think about how you will say no if you are offered illegal drugs. If you have taken drugs already, you need to think carefully about your reasons for doing so, and what the eventual effect might be on you and those you care about. Remember that it is never too late or too early to seek help if you have a problem with drugs.

Institute for the Study of Drug Dependence (ISDD)
Waterbridge House
32-36 Loman Street
London
SE1 0EE
Tel: 0171 928 1211

Narcotics Anonymous
P.O. Box 1980
London
N19 3LS
Tel: 0171 272 9040
National Helpline:
Tel: 0171 498 9005
(10.00-22.00 hrs)

What Can We Do?

ADULTS ALSO NEED TO BE AWARE THAT CHILDREN WILL OFTEN COPY WHAT THEY ARE DOING.

If they see parents or relatives smoking or drinking, or even taking illegal drugs, they may come to think of this as acceptable behaviour.

Children and adults who have read this book together may find it helpful to share their ideas and views on the issues involved. People who are experiencing problems connected with drug use might want to talk to someone who can help. The organisations listed below will be able to provide information and support, both to drug users and their families.

Families Anonymous
Unit 37
Doddington and Rollo
Community Association
Charlotte Despard Avenue
London
SW11 5JE
Tel: 0171 498 4680

The Standing Conference on Drug Abuse (SCODA)
1-4 Hatton Place
Hatton Garden
London
EC1 8ND
Tel: 0171 430 2341

Adfam
Chapel House
18 Hatton Place
London EC1N 8ND
Tel: 0171 405 3923

Turning Point
101 Back Church Lane
London E1 1LU
Tel: 0171 702 2300

Re-solv
30a High Street
Stone
Staffordshire
ST15 8AW
Tel: 01785 817885

Release
388 Old Street
London
EC1V 9LT
Tel: 0171 729 9904
(10.00 - 18.00hrs, Mon-Fri)
Tel: 0171 603 8654 (24 hrs)

Alcohol and Drug Foundation (ADFA)
PO Box 269
Woden Act 2606
Australia
ADFA produces a directory of services related to alcohol and drug problems.

INDEX

addiction 18-20
AIDS 20
alcohol 4, 6 10, 11, 17, 20, 21, 27, 30, 31
amphetamines 10
amyl nitrite 10

barbiturates 10

caffeine 10
cannabis 10, 13, 15, 17, 20, 23
cocaine 11, 15
coffee 4, 6

dealers 8, 17, 23
depressants 10
drugs
　abuse 3, 7, 9, 12-14, 15, 21, 24-26, 27-29, 30
　cocktails 7
　dosage 6
　kinds 4, 7, 11
　medicine 3, 4-6, 7, 10, 11
　on prescription 6, 7, 10
　quality 7, 17, 23

Ecstasy 8, 11, 15, 16, 22, 25

glue sniffing 9, 11, 20, 25

heroin 11

'kicking the habit' 24-26, 27-29

legislation 15, 17
LSD 11, 20

nicotine 11, 15, 18, 27, 30, 31

overdose 15, 23

side-effects 4, 7, 10-11, 12-14, 17, 18, 21-23, 29, 30
solvents 11
steroids 11, 16, 17

tobacco 4, 6, 11, 15, 27, 30, 31
tolerance 4, 6, 11, 15, 27, 30, 31
trafficking 15, 27

withdrawal symptoms 18, 24

Photocredits

All the pictures in this book are by Roger Vlitos apart from pages: 1, 3, 6 bottom, 10 bottom, 14, 15, 17 top, 17 bottom, 23 bottom, 27, 28 top: Frank Spooner; 7: Glaxo. The publishers wish to acknowledge that all of the photographs taken by Roger Vlitos in this book have been posed by models.